MY JOURNEY
PART 1

A FEW OF THE LESSONS AND EXPERIENCES, MY HEAVENLY FATHER TAUGHT ME ALONG THE WAY

APOSTLE SHIRLEY WHARTON

It is our prayer and declaration that you would maintain a Spirit of Integrity concerning the knowledge shared with you in this book. Meaning when using the information in this book publicly, you would give the author, Apostle Shirley Wharton proper recognition and acknowledgement for the knowledge, work, experience, research, and labor of development of this book.

No part of this book may be reproduced by mimeograph process or by another method of duplication unless expressed written permission has been granted by Apostle Shirley Wharton.

Thank You In Advance
for you countenance of righteousness and obedience.

Ecclesiastes 12:14
For God shall bring every work into judgment, with every secret thing, whether it be good or whether it be evil.

First Edition: 2022

ISBN: 978-1-934905-15-9

Worldwide Kingdom Publishing
1911 Horger St
Lincoln Park, Michigan 48146

Copyright 2022 by Apostle Shirley Wharton
All rights reserved.

DEDICATION

I dedicate this book to my Lord & Savior Jesus Christ. For without His love and mercy this story would be entirely different.

Also, to those that in spite of my faults stuck with me and loved me through it all. I thank God for the part that each of you have played in my life. For it has made me the person that I am today.

SPECIAL THANKS

Special thanks first and foremost to my Lord and Saviour "Jesus Christ". You have never failed me. You truly have been with me all the time.

Special thanks to my children: Derrick, Stephanie, Tonya, Timothy and Brian. My three granddaughters Deja, Kennedy, and Gabrielle who help to keep me young. I love you with all my heart.

Special thanks to my "God's Way" family who have my back in prayer.

Special thanks to Jackie White and Anita Thomas (Penny). You stood with me when everyone else walked away.

Special thanks to Dr. Charissee Lewis for helping me to write this book. You truly was a God-send.

Special thanks to my friend, Carla King who

passed away just as I was nearing the end of this book. You were the one who led me to Dr. Lewis and was excited about writing your own book. Love you, my friend and yes, you are missed!

Special thanks to my "Kingdom Konnectors" family under the leadership of Apostle Ramon Clark.

Special thanks to my Tuesday prayer group under leadership of Pastor Sheryl Lloyd and Prophetess Lenora Strange. Thanks for your friendship and prayers.

Special thanks to Apostle Bill & Prophetess Loraine Thornton.

PURPOSE OF BOOK

My purpose in writing this book is first out of obedience to the Holy Spirit. My greatest desire is to please Him, and my instructions was to write a book. My prayer is that as I share parts of my journey with you, that not only will it be a blessing to you, but it will minister to your spirit man that at the turning of every page you will find yourself being healed, delivered, and set free from the strongholds that have held you captive as you cry with me, and yes, even laugh with me on my journey.

INTRODUCTION

Have you ever been betrayed by people you thought were your friends and they turned out to be your biggest enemies? What about your husband, the father of your children who betrayed your trust, even in death? Have you ever been wounded by a spiritual leader maybe your pastor or pastors, who you trusted to watch over your soul, only to find out they could not be trusted, either? Things you shared in confidence was preached over the pulpit, and you knew they were talking about you. Betrayal is a treacherous spirit that is like a cancer that destroys from the inside out. It has destroyed and divided many families, as well as many churches. I have been wounded by this spirit as I am sure many of you have been, also. It caused me to question and look at people differently; but worst than that it caused me to become angry, bitter, and judgmental. Angry, because I felt like a fool knowing everyone saw this person, but me. I kept giving them the benefit of doubt, even putting them over what God was trying to show me. Bitter, because I refused to check myself, and I allowed my heart to become hard. Judgmental, because I became critical of every thing and everyone. It has been said, hurting people hurt others, and that is what I did; I hurt others with my words. For out of the abundance of the heart, the mouth speaks for my heart had become cold and hard. Even so, there is a light at the end of the tunnel and I pray as you read this book that you will find that just as God has healed and delivered me, He will do the same for you. For He is no respecter of persons!

TABLE OF CONTENTS

Dedication
Special Thanks
Purpose of Book
Introduction

Chapter (1):   Insight Into My Childhood
Chapter (2):   Betrayal
Chapter (3):   The Power of the Word
Chapter (4):   Obedience
Chapter (5):   Parable of the Flies
Chapter (6):   Parable of the Truck Driver
Chapter (7):   My First Encounter with the Holy Spirit
Chapter (8):   Releasing Grief
Chapter (9):   Seed of Murder
Chapter (10): Thrust into Ministry
Chapter (11): Right Place Right Time
Chapter (12): The Goodness of God
Chapter (13): Battle for my Life
Chapter (14): Angels Unaware
Chapter (15): The Journey

CHAPTER ONE

INSIGHT INTO MY CHILDHOOD

I grew up in a little small country town called Hopkinsville, Kentucky and I was the only child born to my father and mother for about 4 years when my little sister was born. My father was a farmer and my mother was a beautician. If we were poor we didn't know it, meaning my sister and I. We wore nice clothes, and always had plenty to eat. Christmas, the tree was full of gifts. I went to kindergarten took tap lessons, and through out High School I was in the band and I played the clarinet. I took piano lessons for a while and regret not taking it more seriously.

My mother was the youngest of 10 and one of her sisters died before I was born; but she left 2 boys and 1 girl. As families do, the other siblings took them in and raised them. She was like a 2nd mother to my sister and I. She had gone into the Air Force received a degree, and traveled the world to many far away places. So I decided her dream would be my dream, to finish High School, and go into the Air Force. Well, I finished High School; but did not make it to the Air Force. Toward the end of my last year, I met this young man who was 8 years older than I was and that summer I found out I was pregnant and my life changed for real.

I had already purposed in my heart, that if he did not ask me to marry him before the baby was born; he could forget it and I meant that. He did and I will expound on this later.

We had a son named after him, born with a birth defect. If he had a been born in this time, he would have been classified as a special needs baby. Perfect body, all 5 fingers and toes, but a part of his brain tissue (so I was told) was on the outside like a veil over his eyes. I didn't get to see him; because immediately, he was rushed to Vanderbuilt, Hospital in Nashville, Tennessee. Then my husband came into the room to tell me something was wrong with the baby and even as he spoke, our son was being sent to another hospital. So he left! Leaving me to process this information all by myself. I can remember to this day with tears, turning my face to the wall and crying out to God. I told Him I did not care how he looked, he was mine and that I was going to love him regardless, all I wanted was for Him to allow my son to live. Well, He did!

Some weeks after he was born they told us we could come and pick him up. Neither of us knew what to expect, not to mention I would be seeing my son for the first time since he was born. They gave us a name that to this day we have not been able to pronounce. They said it was rare and the part of the brain that was on the outside was taken off. They didn't know what part of the brain was taken off and how he would be affected. He was left with a small stitch across the bridge of his nose; other than the fact, that his head was about the size of a large grapefruit, he looked like a normal baby. We were given no instructions or medicine. We were told nothing about how to take care of this baby or what to expect. They just handed him to us and said good-bye. I believe that had he been born in this day and time, with technology the way it is, things would have been different, but that was 1965. I was 19 years old, married with a son who with no warnings would have seizures and remained as much a baby as the day he was born. He could not sit up by himself. He could not speak or comprehend anything, as far as we could tell. In 1968, we moved to Detroit right after the riots, so now there was no support at all, both our families were in Kentucky. Talk about growing up fast!

I wanted other children, but my husband was afraid that something would be wrong with them, too. I became pregnant, but I had a miscarriage. That really hurt, but I soon found myself pregnant, again. This time I gave birth to a normal healthy baby boy.

During my pregnancy, Bug (his nickname) seemed to sense that I was pregnant and would cry, constantly. For some reason laying across my lap cuddled around my stomach, he would stop crying. When the baby was born he started crying, too. I was not saved so I knew nothing about the transference of spirits. I was at home everyday by myself with two crying children because my husband worked afternoons. One day, I had the baby in one arm Bug across my lap and I was crying, too. I was at the end of my rope.

One night as I sat on the edge of the bed holding Bug while he cried, in my heart I cried out to God saying, "Lord, I've gone as far as I can go with this." What I did not know was from that very moment, Bug began to die. He still would cry but did not want to eat, I literally had to force him to eat something. It was a Saturday and I was going around the corner to get my hair done. My husband was watching TV, Bug was nice and quiet, laying on the couch and the baby was asleep, when I left.

Coming home every thing was the same except Bug was in his bed; instead of on the couch. Running, to the bathroom all of a sudden I stopped and went into the bedroom and stood there looking at Bug when for no reason at all I picked him up and held him in my arms all the while walking toward the living room where my husband was still caught up in the football game. As I stood there, I said look at Bug, he is sleeping so peaceful that I can't even feel him breathing against me. Finally, he heard what I said as I repeated myself, not even realizing what I was saying. He jumped, looked at him in my arms and said Shirley, Bug's gone as he took off down the backstairs calling out to the older couple who lived downstairs.

When he said, "Bug was gone," I was filled with anger, and talking to Bug I said, "How dare he say that, you're still warm." I had always heard that dead people are cold and all I knew was he was still warm. I noticed his pants were wet so I laid him on the bed, all the time talking to him and telling him Momma's going to change your diaper. I had just gotten the diaper off when the lady from downstairs came in and saw this liquid dripping from him penis and went hollering back downstairs. I continued to talk to Bug telling him I wonder what is her problem? Even when the coroner came and they took him away, on the inside I was convinced they had taken my baby away and he was still alive. The next day we had to go and view the body and only then did I come to the realization that he was gone. Everything I did that day was totally out of character for me. Looking back on my actions, I was on my way to the bathroom, but when I passed by the room he was sleeping in; I just suddenly stopped and went in and stood over his bed, smiling at how peaceful he looked when out of the blue I reached down and picked him up in my arms. I would have never done this, especially since he was finally resting. It was as if I knew without knowing that he was gone, if that makes any sense to you.

Rueben Wharton III was 5 years old when he passed and his brother was 5 months. They were both June babies. Some years later when I had gotten saved, I was talking to the Lord about "Bug" and I asked Him out of curiosity, "Did Bug even know that I was his mother or Rueben was his father?" He could not talk, so we never heard daddy or momma and there was nothing that said he even recognized us, in his eyes or his reactions.

The Lord took me back to when his brother was born and we wanted to take the baby down south so our families could see their new grandson. I could not handle both and one of my husband's cousin told us about a place in

Belleville. After checking everything out, we left him for the weekend. Upon returning to pick him up, one of the nurses asked me, "How do you all take care of him?" I asked her, "What do you mean?" She said, "We could not get his shoes on?" That was the strangest thing to me, but neither could I. When we returned home, I got him ready for bed and the next morning, when I dressed him, his shoes went on like butter. The Lord let me know that, yes, he knew us. He may not have been able to say the words; but he knew the sound of our voice, our touch, our smell, and most of all, our love and his surroundings. His body was reacting the only way he knew how to respond, for being taken out of what was familiar to him, to an atmosphere where nothing was familiar. I am writing this part and crying at the same time when I think of the goodness of God and how mindful He is, of us. He covers all the bases leaving nothing hanging. Remember I told you, when Bug was born and my husband told me the news that he had been rushed to Vanderbilt

Hospital in Nashville; I turned my face to the wall, asking God to just let him live! Well, God revealed to me years later that just as he had allowed him to live, because I had asked Him. He had left it up to me when to take Him. One of my favorite scriptures is **Psalm 27:13**. Where would I be if I had failed to see the goodness of the Lord in the land of the living. God has been good to me, even when I didn't recognize His goodness at the time, He has been good and faithful to me. I can honestly say that not for one second did we regret having Bug. He was our first born and we loved him with all of our heart and neither were we ashamed of him. We were used to the stares of others. There were many days when he fell asleep laying on my husband's chest. If he knew nothing, he knew love. He was the first person I actually loved more than myself. I remember one Easter when my sister and I was young and we lived on 4th street, in Kentucky and my mother made sure we had our Easter outfits new shoes, our little purses, we lacked nothing. For some reason I watched her, come out in the same dress, she had worn many times before and I remember saying to myself, "Why didn't mama get her something new to wear?" Being a mother, now I know the answer to that question. You make sacrifices for the ones you love and you do it willingly.

CHAPTER TWO

BETRAYAL

Betrayal is when someone violates your trust in them. When someone you trust lies on you, cheats on you, abuses you or hurts you by putting their own self-interest first. Betrayal is probably the most devastating loss a person can experience no matter how strong you are, betrayal hurts.

Psalm 55:12-14
For it was not an enemy that reproached me; Then I could have born it: Neither was it he that hated me that did magnify himself against me; Then I would have hid myself from him: But it was thou, a man mine equal, My guide, and mine acquaintance. We took sweet counsel together,

But it's those we grow up with, confide in, sleep next to, share with, eat, and drink with.

Sunday morning, December 24, 1995, (Christmas Eve morning), I awoke to a phone call from Henry Ford Rehabilitation Hospital, which would change the lives of my whole family. My husband had been admitted to the hospital some weeks earlier suffering from a stroke and they were calling to say he had taken a turn for the worst, and for me to come to the hospital. As I jumped out of the bed to get ready I heard the Lord say, "Take the children with you." I called my oldest son and told him I would pick him up on the way. My 2 girls were getting dressed and my second oldest son was still asleep, when in my Spirit I said to myself I'll just let him sleep; but then I heard that voice again, "Take the children with you." I woke him up and we all left headed for the hospital laughing and talking all the way, never once thinking it was anything to serious. They had been having trouble with his blood pressure going up, so I thought they would get it down and he would be okay.

When we arrived they ushered us into this small room, the doctor came in, told us what had happened and then he said, "Mr. Wharton passed about 5 minutes before you got here. The revelation of what the doctor said seemed to hit us all at the same time as one by one my children lost it and I stood there looking from one child to the next in complete shock. For the first time since being a mother I felt completely helpless.

The ride home was the longest ride ever, you could have heard a pin drop. I think we were all in shock and experiencing feelings we did not know what to do with. One thing I think we all knew, was that life as we had known it would never be the same. My youngest son was 11 years old at at the time and had spent the night in Troy, Michigan with a friend. We still had to tell him, his father wouldn't be coming home.

I was always told he wanted to be buried in Kentucky, and if anything happened to him all I had to do was go to Detroit Diesel, his workplace and they would tell me everything I needed to know concerning his insurance. Well, he passed on Christmas Eve, the plant was closed so I had access to nothing including money because the credit union was closed and there was no debit card. The funeral home knew we had insurance so arrangements were made for a small service here and the main service and burial was in his home town, in Kentucky.

I had four children who still lived at home and two of them were totally dependent on me. They were still minors. Remember, I had no money, I needed to get us down south and the church did not offer me any help at all.

I thank God for his faithfulness. **Psalm 46:1** says God is our refuge and strength an ever - present help in trouble, and He showed up.

While I was out making arrangements people stopped by and dropped off cards with money in them which was enough to get us to our destination and back. Look at God! He provided and we owed no man nothing, but to love him. While in Kentucky my oldest son was arrested and he asked me to get him out so he would not have to spend the night in jail. I said I would, but changed my mind when I realized this was all the money I had, we were out of town, I had 2 children depending on me and we still had to get back home. Not to mention, I didn't know when I would have access to some more money. He was upset with me, but at the time he did not understand the position I had been thrust into over night. It wasn't about just him; but all of us.

I married their father at 18 years old. I left my parents house into his house. He had always been the bread winner and I was the stay-at-home mom. Now at age 49, I was the head of the house and everything rested on my shoulders.

When we arrived back home and I was able to go to his job with the death certificate to prove he was deceased, the lady pulled out his files, looked at me and for the first time I learned that the insurance had been taken out of my name and put in the children's name. Looking at my face, she said, "You didn't know did you?" I told her, "I didn't!" She said so many men come in here angry or upset with their wives and want to change the beneficiary on their insurance and I try to talk them out of it. Sitting in that chair, I went through every emotion that you could imagine. When I could finally speak, I said, "Miss, if we had been divorced, or even separated I could understand, but this man was sleeping in our bed, in our house every night and right now I could dig him up, kill him, and bury him all over, again!" She laughed, but I was dead serious. I felt so betrayed, so humiliated, by someone I had been married to for 31 years and had 6 children by.

Since, I couldn't sign the insurance papers, I would have to bring the 3 older children back to sign, because the other 2 were not old enough. I was so emotional and angry. I had to drive around for a while and get my head straight before telling the older children, that they were the beneficiaries of his insurance, not me and they were responsible to pay for his burial, which they did with no problem.

He was buried in Kentucky with our oldest son who passed when he was 5 years old and where his parents were buried. All his wishes was carried out. If I had known about the insurance before hand; I don't know if I would have taken him back to Kentucky to be buried. Just saying. To be honest, it was as if even from the grave his intentions were to hurt me. It wasn't so much what he did; it was how he did it. I was with him, when we signed the papers for the insurance. Months before he passed, I was watching television when there was this ad about insurance, and it was in my spirit to ask him about the insurance. So when we were alone, I said, "Why don't we get the 3 older children together and talk to them about the insurance, so they will know what to do, in case something happens to both of us?" His answer was, "All you have to do is go to the plant and they will tell you everything you need to know." Two other times, I approached him with the same question and the answer was always the same.

A few years later the Lord let me know that was Him giving my husband a chance to get it straight. He was given 3 times to tell me the truth and he chose not to!

Back in Detroit, I found out that everything he had told me was a lie. He told me that if anything happened to him the house would be paid off, that was a lie. The car would be paid for, that was a lie, and the car was repossessed.

Usually, when someone passed we would take up an offering for them, but that wasn't the case with me and when I asked to borrow some money until my money came in, I was told that the Lord said, "No!" I told them I had the money, I just had to wait for them to send it to me, still the answer was, no! It hurt, but after all was said and done the Lord let me know that He didn't want them to give me anything. I didn't know then; but God was breaking all ties between them and me and the answer really was, no!

I went to bible study at Church, the week we returned home: and boy was I in for a rude awakening. Everyone was waiting on me and I was told I was full of the devil, that I had killed my husband and every spirit that you could name, I had it. They had me so messed up that if they had told me I had flown to the Vatican and killed the pope I would have believed them.

I came home, sat on the bed in a state of utter confusion and I said to the Lord, "How did I become so evil and I didn't know it? In my brokenness, the Lord began to minister to me. He said everything she told you, you were, she is. It was like looking at a movie as the Lord began to show me her true self and the root of everything was jealousy. That was hard for me to conceive because looking at the outside she was the complete package. Thank God, He judges the inside and not the outside.

I Samuel 16:7
But the Lord said to Samuel, "Do not look at his appearance or at his physical stature, because I have refused him. For the Lord does not see as man sees," for man looks at the outward appearance, but the Lord looks at the heart."

CHAPTER THREE

THE POWER OF THE WORD

It was Easter, Sunday 1996 I went to church and every one was sitting on one side of the church; I and my youngest son sat on the opposite side, alone. I was told there were so many demon spirits around me that I had to be separated from the rest of the people. I wasn't thinking clearly at that time; or I would have told them that since they were so righteous and holy, why were they separating themselves from me from the demons they said, I had? "Why not just cast them out?" I felt so alone, but I felt I had to be strong for my son. I could not let him see me breakdown. When I saw my 2 daughters walking in, I got up, and asked them to take my youngest son home without any explanation. Even when they asked me, "Why and where was I going?" I could not let them see how distraught I was, plus I did not trust myself to say anything without breaking down and crying. I needed to be alone. I needed some answers. I left church and checked myself into a hotel and laid there in a fetal position all night; not knowing of anyone I could pick up the phone and call and talk to. I just felt like everyone I knew had forsaken me and I was all alone.

The following morning I heard the Holy Spirit say call "Penny." I picked up the phone and called not even knowing what to expect. Out of everybody in the church, she was the only one who stood with me even to this day. The Lord always has a ram in the bush, and boy did I need one.

I found out later that my friend and Pastor had gone to everyone we knew here in Detroit and even called down South telling everyone that we knew, that I was the devil. There was another friend that we had in common. The Lord brought her before me and I was impressed to call her. She said I could come over and I found out that our mutual friend had been to her house twice to convince her how evil I was. She was skeptical but she let me in and to this day we are still friends. Thank you, Jackie White! She has had my back more times than I can count.

Not being in that atmosphere, having them lay hands on me, and praying for me; things began to clear up and that's when I really began to form a true relationship with the Lord.

As I said, I was so messed up that I was even afraid to pray. For they had told me I was praying witchcraft prayers, because my spirit was evil. I believed what they said, so I didn't trust myself to pray. There was so much coming against me; that for the first time in my life, I considered suicide. I was in a dark place and the enemy was talking; but so was the Holy Spirit and He won. As I sat at the foot of my bed, He brought my children before me, and He said, "Who's going to love them like you?

Who's going to pray for them like you would if you are gone?" That woke me up and to this day suicide has never been an option for me.

I called TBN begging them to pray for my salvation, because for the 1st time I doubted I was saved. I remembered the woman on the other line saying, "Miss, you confessed Christ you are saved." I could tell that even she was getting frustrated with me. I had this book called Prayers that Availeth Much. I began every day, reading the prayers out loud and I watched nothing, but Christian TV not realizing God was doing a marvelous work in me.

I was sitting at my dining room table shortly after leaving the church when the phone rang. It was a voice I had not heard in a while, but was well familiar with. When I went to say something, I was told to shut-up and listen. When she said that, since I had company I started getting up from the table and heading to the back of the house. By the time I reached my bedroom, she had said what she called to say which was "You are cursed from, the top of your head to the soles of your feet." Before she could say anything else, the prayers I had been reading rolled up out of me like a thunder bolt, and I heard myself say with an authority I didn't know that was in me. "You can't curse me - I've been redeemed by the blood of the lamb," and before I could say anything else, she slammed the phone down so hard, I wouldn't be surprised if it didn't break. God delivered me that day and she never called my house, again. The Shirley that left her church that Easter Sunday feeling lost and rejected was not the same Shirley. I had been changed from the inside - out. I truly was a new creature in Christ Jesus. The devil thought he had me, but God had a plan far bigger than I could see at the time. The enemy's goal was to literally kill me. I was wearing a size 5 suit at the time and I had to pin it up at the waist. God's plan was for me to live and declare the works of the Lord and His plan prevailed. St John 10:10, we forget the enemy comes to steal, kill, and destroy and it is God that comes to give us life and that more abundantly. I say it was her church, because it definitely was not God's church. I know, I was in it and I know the spirit that was behind it and it wasn't the Holy Spirit.

CHAPTER FOUR

OBEDIENCE

I Samuel 15:22 reads, "To obey is better than sacrifice and to hearken than the fat of rams." The enemy would have us believe we are the only ones to have been wronged, which leaves us open to a root of bitterness. Yes I was hurt, but I also hurt others. As the saying goes, "hurting people hurt other people." I had this friend at the old church and I ignored all the warnings and allowed bitterness to set up in my heart. When the Lord put a finger on the resentment, and the anger, and unforgiveness. I didn't deal with it. I prophesied to her out of that bitterness and I hurt her to the point, she left the church.

I came home one day from work, sat down on the sofa and immediately the Lord began to talk to me. Some time had passed, and the Lord had dealth with my heart. He told me to call

(Doris) not her real name. I said, "Lord I'm the last person she wants to hear from." Again, he said call (Doris). This time I picked up the phone and called. She answered and I told her how sorry I was and that it had noting to do with her. I shared with her what God had shared with me. To my surprise she told me she already knew because, the Lord had dealt with her, also. We talked for about an hour and there was nothing between us, but love. She was going to call me and set up a date when we could meet within about 2 or 3 weeks. Later, I received the news she had passed. To this day, I thank God that He gave me the opportunity to set things right. I think all the time, "What if I had not obeyed?" I did not know she only had a few weeks to live, but God did. It has been over 20 years and I still can not thank God enough for His mercy towards me.

I Corinthians 15:58
Therefore, my dear brothers and sisters, stand firm. Let nothing move you. Always give yourselves fully

to the work of the Lord, because you know that your labor in the Lord is not in vain.

Everybody wants to be used by God. I was saved, young in the Lord and I had been praying to be used by God. The Lord answered my prayer and even though I was obedient, the Pastor stood up in front of everyone and really hurt my feelings. Being young in the Lord, it was hard for me to understand how the people you looked up to and respected were the ones to hurt you. Boy, did I have a lot to learn!

I came home that night and I had a little talk with Jesus. I told Him, that if being used by God was going to be like this, He could have it! He answered by withdrawing His Spirit from me. I quickly repented and I told Him whatever He gave me to do, I would do it; and whatever He gave me to say, I would say it and immediately His Spirit returned to me. Looking back, that had to be at least 46 years ago, give or take a few years. The message I received that day was …if I really wanted to be used by God, it had to be His way. I couldn't pick and choose what I would or would not do. I was either all in or not at all. So how did I find myself at this place for a second time? **Habakkuk 2:2** says to write the vision and make it plain that all who hear it may run with it. The vision God gave me was founded on **Titus 2:3-5**, where God says that the older women are to teach the younger women. The vision started with a concern, as I began to look at our young women and the difference in today's women and the women of my generation. My heart became grieved as I watched our young girls whose only identity is in a man. Women willing to sacrifice their integrity, having babies out of wedlock by any man that will say those 3 magic words, "I love you!" Women settling for anything, because they believe they don't deserve any better.

When a man can beat you, put you in the hospital, spit in your face, call you all kinds of ungodly names and you are willing to accept that and call it "love", something is wrong with that picture.

Even in the church women are beaten down and made to feel less then. Scriptures have been taken out of context to silence women. Especially **I Timothy 2:12**, but I suffer not a woman to teach, nor to usurp authority over the man, but to be in silence. It's hard to believe, but even today there are pastors who believe that God did not call women to ministry.

What's going to happen to the next generation if we the older women do not rise up and start teaching our young girls that our identity comes from God and not man.

The vision is to give women back their identity. You are more than somebody's wife or mother. We must know who we are to fulfill the purposes that God has called us to walk in.

I know this vision was from God and not just a good idea, because it was birthed through prayer. I put in the work, I went through the process. I prayed. I waited on God for the right season and His timing.

I went to my pastor at the time, told him the vision and what God wanted me to do. I am a firm believer that if you are under somebody's else leadership you should go to them and let them know what you believe God is saying; rather than them hearing it from someone else. It's a matter of respect. When I went in to share my vision I was on cloud 9, when I came out I felt deflated. Like a balloon that someone had let all the air out of. He felt that my vision would keep the people from coming to church even though, I told him it was one night out of the month and not a service night. When I arrived home I sat down and began to cry out to the Lord. I told Him that I felt like a rock between a hard place. I said, "Your word says to obey those in authority over you so maybe

I'm not supposed to do anything. The Lord never spoke but He sure did answer, because like a vacuum He with drew His Spirit from me, again. It did not take me but a second to get the message, for if you remember this was the second time this had happened to me. This time He let me now that the vision was not about me that this was His vision and as I once again repented His Spirit returned. I learned later that yes we are to obey those who have the rule over us; but not if it goes against what God is saying. He is the final authority.

I went to church that Sunday and the Pastor got up and announced over the pulpit that I would be having a meeting for Women at my house. Surprise! Surprise! I did not have to say or do anything, God did it. All He wanted was for me to come into agreement with His plan.

Friday, April 27, 2007 I had the 1st Women's meeting in my home. At the time of our 1st meeting, the only thing I knew was the vision was for women and that I was in the will of God. I did not even have a name. Everyone kept asking me what is the name and all I would say is that God haven't given me one yet. The pressure continued about the name and the answer was always the same. I knew in my spirit the name had to come from God, after all He said it was His vision.

Finally, Monday, November 10, 2008, God gave me the name for His vision. I was sitting in my favorite chair in the living room when up out of my belly. I heard "Nurturing Women." It was so real and audible that I looked down at my stomach and I said, "Nurturing Women?" I heard again, "Nurturing Women" and I knew that was to be the name of the vision.

I want to say to you who may have an opportunity to read this book. If God has entrusted you with His vision do not allow anyone to pressure you into going ahead of God. Everybody has an opinion about what you should or should not do. Remember, if God gave it to you, He is holding you responsible for it.

I was tested in everything God told me to do and criticized about how I did things. I learned early you can not tell everybody everything and you can't please everybody, either; but you can please God. Everybody's not going to like you, let alone love you. So if you are expecting everybody to be in your corner you're already deceived. I was also being tested by the Holy Spirit to see if I could be trusted with His vision or would I fail the test and choose to please man. Thank God, I chose to please God.

We were in my basement about 2 years when the Holy Spirit spoke to me about a breakfast. I remember saying a breakfast? My first thought was we do not have any money for a breakfast. We met the last Friday of every month and no offerings were taken. After withdrawing His Spirit from me twice, I was determined there wouldn't be a 3rd time. I told the young ladies that were with me what God had said and I set out looking for a place to have a breakfast. I did not know what I was looking for; but I knew I would know it when I saw it. One of the ladies told me about a church near her home and how beautiful one of the rooms were. The minute I saw it; I knew this was the place. The Lord had given me specific instructions on how He wanted the breakfast to be. The room was to be set up like a wedding reception. The colors were to be Gold and White. Gold symbolizing the refinement of the Spirit; royalty, and transcendence **Revelation 21:21, Proverbs 25:11-12.** White symbolizing triumph, victory in conflict, righteousness and purity. It also speaks of holiness, and success, **Revelation 7:9; 19:14.** Real china, silverware, tables set up with real linen table cloths and napkins. Programs and tickets printed out, everything had to be done in a spirit of excellence. We had vendors, plus we drew names and gave gifts that cost more than your ticket. The food was catered and it was presented in a spirit of excellence. Eventually, catfish was added to the menu and there were some women who wanted to bring their husbands. We turned no one away, even if they could not buy a ticket, they were still welcome.

After our first breakfast, I breathed a sigh of relief that everything went so smooth and God met every need. As I stood there alone, this woman walked up to me expressing how much she enjoyed herself and she couldn't wait for the next year so she could come to the next one. When she walked away I said, "Lord, You mean I have to do this again?" Little did I know, there would be 10 more to go and it would grow from 100 to 300. The lessons I learned are priceless. I learned to trust God in ways that I had never had to trust Him before. Remember, there was only 7 of us and that included me, and we had no money. I learned to keep the vision on Him, reminding Him of what He told me, **I Peter 5:7**, "Casting all your care upon Him; for He careth for you." The vision was His and He would make provision for the vision and He did every time.

Many times, He laid it on the heart of others to sow into the breakfast. I thank God for their obedience, to the vision. Breakfast number "9" as I sat in the office to write the final check to cover all the expenses for the breakfast; we were over a thousand dollars short. The enemy was saying, you do not have the money you need to cancel, but I knew in my spirit to write the check that God did not bring us this far to let us down. I handed the woman the check and she gave me my receipt. We left not knowing how God was going to work this out, but I can tell you this, before we went to bed that night the check was covered, my faith was taken to a whole new level that day as God honored His word.

As we prepared for breakfast number 10, I told the ladies that while I was praying the Lord had said this would be our last breakfast at "Fellowship Chapel". The way He said it left me thinking that 2019 the breakfast would be at a different location, since He did not say why. Of course now, we know it would be, because we would be in a pandemic and everything would be shut down.

Because of what had happened the last breakfast with the money, I said in my heart that this would probably not happen again; especially since I had passed the test, the last time. Boy, was I wrong. This time we were even shorter than the last time, but God had prepared me to stand the test. As I sat there with the pen in my hand to write the check I said, "Lord, you know what I'm going to do - I'm going to write this check! I was saying to Him, you said this was Your vision and You would make provision for the vision. I took the responsibility off of me and put it back on Him. I remember Him saying to me *"Today you are believing Me for thousands; but the day will come when you will believe me for millions."* Needless to say, the check was covered. If He can't trust us with the little, how will He ever be able to trust us with much.

CHAPTER FIVE

"PARABLE OF THE FLIES"

I was praying and asking the Holy Spirit for a word for our Nurturing Women's Meeting for the following Friday, and so far I had not heard anything. I got up and went to work and on my return home, my picture window was full of flies. I checked all the windows and spent over and hour killing flies. The next day, I came home only to find the picture window full of flies, again. I went through the same routine again checking every window trying to find out how they were getting in and I could find nothing. All I could think of was that flies was one of the plagues in Egypt, and Lord what were You trying to tell me? The 3rd day I came home and there were the flies, again. This time I was almost in a panic as I ran from room to room checking the same windows, again. This time as I ran upstairs and as I put my hands on the window it went up. From all appearances, the window looked closed, but it had slipped down and to the naked eye it looked closed. The Lord said, "Are there any cracks in your foundation?" All the enemy needs is a crack and he will come in and before you know it, he will have taken over. This is why it is so important that we guard our ear gates and that we are selective to what we watch. You can not unsee something, once you have seen it. Looks are deceiving, but we forget that God is all seeing as well as, all knowing. Every time we step outside the will of God, it causes a crack in our foundation. Just because you don't see it, does not mean it is not there. We can not play on the devil's territory. Without the Holy Spirit, you are no match for the enemy. If you play with fire, eventually you are going to get burnt. I hate flies, but I thank God for the lessons He taught me that day. We cannot afford to slip in praying, in reading the word, or anything else that will affect our relationship with God, or just like that window the enemy will have come in and you won't even know how he got in.

I have learned to ask God the hard questions about myself. After all who knows me better than He does. One of my prayers is that He will allow me to see myself through His eyes and accept what He reveals to me. Sometimes we pray and ask God to show us, (us) and when He does; we act like God has it wrong.

Jeremiah 17:9
The heart is deceitful above all things and desperately wicked: who can know it?

God has delivered me from a spirit of jealousy, anger, root of bitterness; just to name a few. So I am constantly checking to make sure those big foxes that I have been delivered from have not crept back in.

We take better care of our cars and homes than we do our spirit. Why is it that we are in better tune to our cars than our spirit man?

CHAPTER SIX

"PARABLE OF THE TRUCK DRIVER"

The Summer after the passing of my husband, there was a family reunion held in Kentucky on his side of the family. My youngest daughter, my youngest son, and I decided to go. I rented a SUV and we set out. It was late when we left, because I had to work that day, pack, also make sure everything was taken care of at home. To make a long story short I was tired. I started out driving when after a few hours an unusual tiredness came over me and I told my daughter she would have to drive. We exchanged places and I remember her asking me which way to go and me telling her to just drive. I remember nothing else. Just as I had suddenly fallen into a coma-like sleep; hours later I suddenly woke up. Even though it was pitch black outside, nothing looked familiar, so I asked my daughter where were we? She said, "I don't know, you just said drive." Well, I could not argue with that! So I told her to come up on the next exit. It was dark, the area was very rural and there was this one gas station that was lit up; so I pulled in and told my daughter to lock the doors for there was no one around that remotely looked like us. I went inside and I asked the man behind the counter could he tell me, where Hopkinsville, Kentucky was and he said he had never heard of the place. You can imagine how I felt, but then he said, there is a truck driver outside and he can tell you how to get there. I thanked him and sure enough there was this one truck driver standing all alone. I walked over to him, told him where I wanted to go and asked him could he tell me how to get to Hopkinsville, Kentucky? He reached into his truck, pulled out this big map, pointed to where we were and told me to go up to the light make a right and if I stayed on that road it would take me to my destination. I started out following his directions which was a 2 lane country road.

The minute I got on the road within 5 minutes, a fog came up that was so thick, I could only see directly right in front of me and that was where the headlights shined. Just like suddenly the fog came up, immediately I was in Warfare. It was like the devil was on one side saying turn around, the truck driver lied. How do you know you are not being set up? God was on the other side reminding me what the truck driver said that if I stay on this road, I'll reach my destination. The children were asleep and not one car was on that road; I was the only one. When I tell you, I saw nothing; I saw nothing. I sat straight up with my eyes completely focused on the road, ahead. This went on for hours and finally I could see day breaking. I have never been so happy to see the sun begin to break through the clouds in my life. About an hour or so later, there was this sign letting me know I had been on the right road and I had reached my destination. Thank You, Jesus!

In 2011, I was ordained as a Pastor. The last thing I wanted to be was a Pastor. To be honest, I didn't want the responsibility. With my mouth, I said ok; but my heart was not in it. Finally the Lord intervened, and told me that until I could embrace it: I would never be able to walk in it. That got my attention and I quickly came into alignment with who God said I was. **Matthew 18:20** says, "For where two or three are gathered together in my name, there I am in the midst of them." The heart and the mouth must agree.

Now I want to take you back to the parable of the truck driver. The incident with the truck driver happened in 1996 and I was ordained as a Pastor in 2011, 15 years later. My daughter and I would often, laugh about how I woke up and asked her where were we? She said, "I don't know you just said, drive!" Normally from my house to Kentucky, would take us about 8 hours; and she had driven almost that far but in the wrong direction. To this day, I don't know where we were, but it took me about 8 hours to get to Kentucky from where we were. Over 15 years later, the Lord let me know that He had planned the whole trip and nothing that happened that night was a coincidence. He said it wasn't an accident that we came up on that particular exit. He was the truck driver and the map the truck driver pulled out represented His word. It was not by chance that I fell in such a deep sleep. In fact, He let me know while writing this book that he put me to sleep because He knew I would need that rest for the warfare I was going to encounter. Twenty-five years later I received this revelation God has a time and a season for everything. I call this parable the gift that keeps on giving, because I never know what He is going to reveal next. I learned if I stay focused and don't allow the enemy to distract me with his lies, but follow the leading of the Holy Spirit. I will always reach my destination. We thought we were lost but according to the Lord, we were exactly where He wanted us to be. We were not lost to Him. This is a lesson for all of us. The enemy will do everything possible to get our attention off of Jesus. He comes with distractions and he will contradict everything the Lord has told you. My instructions were clear. Just stay on this road and you will reach your destination. He is saying the same thing to us today.

Matthew 7:14

Enter by the narrow gate: for wide is the gate and broad is the way that leads to destruction, and there are many who go in by it.

There is a narrow road that leads to life and a broad road that leads to destruction, and if you stay focus and stay on the narrow road you will reach your destination, too. The "choice is yours!"

CHAPTER SEVEN

MY FIRST ENCOUNTER WITH THE HOLY SPIRIT

Going back to my childhood, it seems as if I have always known there was a God and would talk to Him about things that concerned me. I remember one day playing in the street, when all of a sudden this cloud came down in front of me forming the heads of 3 people. If I had to say how old I was, I would say around 11 or 12 years old. I remember my father was standing on the front porch. There were other kids playing and there was a lady coming down the street behind me on her way home from work. How I knew this, I don't know, but I did. The cloud was so thick that I could not see through it to the other side and it crossed the road blocking off every thing to the other side. The lady that was coming behind me kept walking and went right through the cloud as if the cloud was not there. It disappeared as quickly as it had formed and I could see the lady continuing on down the road. I realized then, that no one saw this, but me. At the time, I never told anyone what I saw, but I do know that I saw what I saw and when I got saved I asked God about it and all I received was that the three heads represented the Father, the Son, and the Holy Spirit.

One day, I was next door with some other kids from the neighborhood when this lady started telling us about the Lord. To be honest, I really was not paying attention until she said, "In hell you never burn up, you burn forever." There was a seed sown in my heart that day; that hell was not for me and I was not going! I always thought like a piece of paper you will burn up and that's that; but this really changed my perspective about what hell was like. I couldn't get over that burning forever.

CHAPTER EIGHT

RELEASING GRIEF

Friday, December 3, 2021, I was sitting before the Lord when all of a sudden there was this overwhelming urge to embrace my oldest son the one that I told you about earlier that passed when he was 5 years old. I so longed to hug him one more time. My arms literally ached to hold him. It was so powerful I began to cry and I mean uncontrollably. When I could I asked the Lord, "What is this? What's happening?" I heard Him say, "You never had the chance to grieve him." I was too through. When I thought about it, I had to agree. Bug was 5 years old when he passed and I had a 5 month old to take care of, who was the complete opposite of Bug. Wherever I placed Bug is where he stayed. Now I had someone I had to watch every second. I couldn't prop him up and expect him to stay put, he was into everything. It was as if I laid down one child to pick up another. Fifty-one years later I grieved my son. God is so amazing. After all this time, I didn't even know I needed to grieve, but God did!

In September of 1987, I received the news that my first cousin had passed. This was the cousin that went to the Air Force, that I had so wanted to follow in her footsteps. She lived in Georgia was a school teacher and when she didn't show up for school; they sent someone to check on her and she had passed. Upon learning the news, a few of us all went to Georgia to make arrangements and pack up some things in her house.

One night as we all sat around her dining room table, I had what I will call an out of body experience. All of a sudden, my spirit went to another place and I felt her loneliness, her sadness, the disappointments, the unhappiness all the things she felt living in that house. Her husband was killed in Vietnam. She had no children and she never remarried. Just as quick as this happened, it was over and no one knew about the experience I had just had.

I remember as a young child just before he left for Vietnam, they were laughing, playing around couldn't keep their hands off of one another. She was so happy anticipating the children they would have one day. Now here I sat in her house many years later feeling so empty, as I experienced her dreams and expectations for a future that was never fulfilled. I didn't know what the doctor's diagnosis cause of death was, but I believe she died from a broken heart.

CHAPTER NINE

THE SEED OF MURDER

My sister and I did not grow up watching my parents fight and call one another all kinds of names. But this one particular day, all hell broke loose in our house. I remember curling up at the front door not knowing what to think; but in my heart I knew it was my father's fault. I made a vow that day. I vowed that if I ever married a man and he treated me this way; I would kill him, and I meant every word. I was traumatized that day, but since I was only around 6 years old. I did not know that. I also did not know that a spirit of murder entered into my heart that day and as I grew so did that seed. When I found out years later that I was pregnant and he asked me to marry him, I said, "Yes I love you, but if I catch you messing up on me I will kill you!" The words just rolled right off my tongue without me even thinking about it.

A few years later when we moved to Detroit, he was working every day including weekends and overtime. I was stuck in the house, without transportation or any friends. This particular weekend he was off and promised me we would do something together. I was like a kid in a candy store, so looking forward to the weekend. Well, the day came and he did not come home, and when he did; he was drunk and it was too late to go anywhere. He stumbled back to the bedroom and fell asleep on the bed. I was upset, but there was noting I could do about it. I picked up his jacket off the chair so I could hang it up when I reached into his pocket and pulled out a motel ticket. All I remember is when I picked it up; it was as if I picked up a hot coal and it actually burned in my hand, when this happened, something came over me and I was like a zombie on a mission. I walked into the bedroom where he lay on the bed, knocked out. I saw this vase on the chest, and it was one of those hard vases that you put one rose in; I picked it up and walked to the bed. I stood over him and just as I raised it up and was about to bring it down over his head, I heard these words, "Let him that is without sin cast the first stone." **John 8:7**. At the sound of those words, I came to my senses something broke in me and I felt the anger that had been driving me, go out of my body starting from the top of my head down my body and out through my feet. I then turned as in slow motion retracing my steps. I put the vase back on the chest and backed out of the room. He never knew how close he came to dying that night. I understand first hand when people say it was as if something took them over. It was as if, it wasn't me; I did it, but it wasn't me. When I got saved the Lord revealed to me the steps that led to what happened that day. He told me a seed of murder was planted when I was 6 years old and made that vow that came straight from my heart that I would kill the man that treated me this way, and as I grew so did that seed lying dormant all this time waiting for an opportunity to manifest itself that was step one.

Years later, when I was proposed to I said yes, but out of my mouth I added; but if I catch you messing up on me I will kill you, that was step two. Step three came when I stood over him with a vase in my hand with every intention of killing him. The Lord told me, "You made a vow what you would do in your heart, later you spoke it into the atmosphere; and now the only step left was to carry it out. If not but for the grace of God, I would probably be locked up in somebody's prison for murder. Be careful what you vow, especially in anger. You will reap what you sow. The enemy tried to change the plans God had for me even before I knew He had a plan and a purpose for my life. I didn't know Jeremiah 29:11,

Jeremiah 29:11
I know the plans I have for you declares the Lord, plans to prosper you and not to harm you. Plans to give you a hope and a future.

CHAPTER TEN

THRUST INTO MINISTRY

The word thrust means - push (something or someone) suddenly or violently in a specified direction. Push or propel.

In 2009 a friend called to tell me that she and another one our friends were going to enroll in a school called, API. "Apostles, Prophets, Institute", located in Roseville, Michigan. The question was what about me, did I want to enroll, too? I had never heard of API, I didn't know anything about API and to be honest I didn't want to know anything about API. School was the last thing on my mind and even though I tried to dismiss the thought it stayed with me. So, I decided to call the school, let them tell me that the class was full, then I would be off the hook. Well to make a long story short, they had plenty of room and I found myself enrolled in API with deans Dr.

Linnie and Pastor Zonita Swanigan. When the Lord kept telling me that I was being thrust into ministry, I would never have guessed going to school would have been one of the doors He opened. I was the oldest in my class, I was not computer savvy and I had not typed since I was in High School. Lord what am I doing here? Well, I soon found out. API stretched me in ways that I didn't even think possible, but it was the best thing that could have happened to me.

Since being saved I've been in a lot of churches over the years and under a lot of different leaders, men and women. Some of the experiences I've had was not the best and with some I left feeling betrayed and wounded, but thanks be to God, He worked it all out for my good. I just did not know at the time that was what He was doing.

API prepared me for the ministry He had called and anointed me to do. It took me completely out of my comfort zone. I know beyond a shadow of doubt that API was God's plan for me.

I want to take this time to say "Thank You" to Dr. Linnie and Pastor Z for something they do not even realize they did for me or that I needed. **Matthew 7:16** tells us that we would be known by the fruit we bare. You and Pastor Z were the first to model what a real leader is at all times. There was no competition, no envy, or jealousy. Speaking for myself, I knew you wanted the best for me and you have supported me 100%.

I graduated API in 2013 with a Bachelors degree and the fruit has never changed. When I call or text, I know what I am going to get, because the fruit continues to remain the same. Speaking about support, they were there to support me when I started "Nurturing Women", they were there when I was ordained as a Pastor and they were the ones to ordain me as an Apostle. Everything major in my life they have been there.

God knew what He was doing when He sent me to you. You are people of integrity and your fruit is good. I love and appreciate you, both.

In 2018 10 of us, family and friends went to visit my youngest son who was stationed in Honolulu, Hawaii. We had finally reached the half way mark and as we boarded the plane for the last time. I found myself seated in the back of the plane with the toilets. You can already guess, I was not happy at all and I was murmuring, grumbling, and complaining. What I didn't know was that God had a plan and I was being setup.

When they announced we were getting ready to land; all of a sudden the man that was sitting in front of me with 2 teenage sons, suddenly stood up, turned around and looking straight at me started to rant about how some man, his son was working for had said something inappropriate to his son, and he did not know who he was messing with. He told me he was going to get revenge, and when he said that, I finally got a chance to speak and I said real low and calm, "Sir, if I were you, I'd leave that alone. Vengeance belongs to the Lord." He responded angrily, "I'm not going to leave it alone," and he took off to the front of the plane with his 2 sons, following. My oldest daughter who was sitting behind me said, "Mama leave that man alone, he's crazy and I remember saying to her, "I know what I'm doing," but really I didn't. When we all got up to get off the plane there was a lady sitting across the aisle who walked over to me and said, "I see you are a woman of God." She gave me her card, told me she and her husband were pastors; and if I could, "Would I come to her church the following Sunday?" To be honest in all the excitement, I forgot all about that woman. The next morning as I woke up and went out on the balcony, looking up to the heavens was an experience in itself. I have never seen anything so beautiful. It was as if I could reach up and touch heaven. It was then that the Lord bought what happened on the plane back to me. He let me know it was all a divine set-up. I told my best friend what the Lord had said and what had happened on the plane. I didn't know exactly what the Lord had planned; but I knew I was to go to that church the following Sunday. The enemy tried to block the plan of God, but he lost. There were some things that as Pastors the wife had been praying and asking God for some answers and that day God had sent me all the way from Detroit, Michigan to Honolulu, Hawaii to answer every concern she had. He dotted every "i" and crossed every "t". That's the God we serve. If He has to send someone or send you halfway across the world an answer to your prayers; He will do just that! They knew the Lord had to reveal the things that I was saying, because I knew nothing about them or their church and vice-versa. Look at the divine set-up here. We all had a place in God's plan; yes, even the man who was sitting in front of me. God can and will use whosoever He will.

CHAPTER ELEVEN

RIGHT PLACE RIGHT TIME

Being at the right place at the right time is so important. After graduating from API in 2013, I wanted to take a class in spiritual counseling; but after 4 years I did not want to drive all the way back to Roseville to do it. A friend told me about a couple who graduated from Destiny School of Ministry who were doing Christian Counseling and it was only 10-15 minutes from my house. We decided to enroll and one of our teachers, Dr. Majorie asked Carla and I to go with her to a taping she was doing. To be honest neither of us knew what we were going for other than to support her. She introduced us to Min. Bell and his lovely wife. He explained to us what Dr. Marjorie did and then turned to us and said, now you have your own show. Our eyes could not have gotten any bigger, or our mouths any wider if we tried. I drove all the way back home with both of us in complete shock wondering what just happened? Never in my wildest dream had I even considered being on TV. I believe God did not let us hear the reason we were going, because we would have said "No." After introducing us to TV, Dr. Marjorie was not seen at the school any more. It was as if her assignment was to get us on TV and then she was gone.

I worked with Dr Marjorie on her show for about a year, when I felt in my spirit it was time to start my own program called "Do the Right Thing!"

I am a firm believer that when God opens a door for you, it is for you to open that same door for someone else. It has been about 8 years now and during that time, I have been blessed to give that opportunity to others, who like me had not considered TV.

CHAPTER TWELVE

THE GOODNESS OF GOD

My mother passed October 7, 1976 at the young age of 63. I found out earlier that year that she had been diagnosed having breast cancer. I took the kids, a friend of mine and we drove down to see her. She had loss weight, but she was not bed ridden and was still able to get around. She asked me to comb her hair and as I combed; I was shocked to find more hair in my hands then what was left on her head. I would not say anything: nor would I allow her to see on my face, how I really felt. I tried to act as normal as possible.

The next morning I awoke to this strange sound. I laid there for a minute then sat up moving in the direction of the sound. It was coming from my mother's room and as I opened her bedroom door to check on her the smell of cancer hit me, that raw flesh where they had taken off one of her breast was overwhelming. She was in so much pain that all she could do was make these animal like sounds. She looked at me as I stood over her bed, and you could see the pain in her eyes and the look on her face; as if she was begging me to please do something, anything. I took off out of her room and ran to get my anointing oil out of my purse. I had been saved about three years then, so I did what I knew. I stood over her bed and raised the bottle of oil letting the oil drop down on her as I prayed. I can not even tell you what I said, but this one thing I do know is, that God did a miracle that day. My mother rose up out of that bed smiling and the pain was gone. She spent the rest of the day on the phone calling everyone she knew letting them know how we prayed and she was no longer in pain. In fact, some of her friends told her to send us to their houses to pray for them and we did. The whole time we were there she experienced no pain and she was able to eat! To God be the Glory!

When I received the news that my mom had passed, I had a hard time understanding what had happened. I told the Lord, "I know I didn't doubt you. I know I stood in faith trusting you to heal my mother." The Lord so gently said, "Shirley she had a will, too; and she willed to go. I could not go against her will." At that moment, something her husband said when he called me to tell me she had passed, came to my Spirit and I remember him saying that my mother said she was tired, she gave up, and threw up her hands.

Yes, my mother faithfully went to church and served in the church. She also made sure we went to church. But we all know going and serving in the church does not make you saved.

One night I had this dream that I opened this door and when I peeked in; the room was all lite up and everything was in gold and white. Very majestic looking. I know there was furniture in the room, but my focus was on the bed in the room. I was drawn to the bed and the closer I got I could see there was a baby lying on the bed. The body was that of a new born baby; but the head was my mother's (end of the dream). I knew that was the Lord letting me know my mother was born again. She made it in, that had been a concern for me. Thank God for His Goodness!

Genesis 4:8-10
And Cain talked with Abel his brother: and it came to pass, when they were in the field, that Cain rose up against Abel his brother, and slew him. And the Lord said unto Cain, Where is Abel thy brother? And he said, I know not: Am I my brother's keeper? And he said, What hast thou done? The voice of thy brother's blood crieth unto me from the ground.

I had never been to Mississippi before, but in 2018 I traveled with my daughter to Lorman, Mississippi to enroll her daughter and my granddaughter in "Alcon University" to attend college there. The school is located in a secluded rural area and it's a trip just to go to a dollar store.

My daughter was driving and all was quiet when I had the strangest experience. While on those back wooded roads I heard in my spirit: the souls of the dead crying out for all the injustices that had been done to them down through the years, and it was coming up from the earth. The beatings, the hangings I could imagine it all and I literally wanted to weep and sob for all the things that had been done. God sees and knows everything, nothing escapes Him.

Cain thought no one saw or knew he had killed his brother; but God did.

Matthew 10:29
Not even a sparrow falls to the ground without God knowing it.

Are we not more valuable than a sparrow? I'm sure there are bodies buried out there from centuries ago, but that day, God allowed me to hear the voices of their blood crying out from the earth. "Gone, but not forgotten". This happened more than once and I knew this was God allowing me to experience this.

CHAPTER THIRTEEN

BATTLE FOR MY LIFE

I awoke early one morning in intense pain. My stomach was cramping and I headed toward the bathroom; thinking it was something that I had eaten. It hurt so bad that I couldn't even think. The house was quiet every one was asleep except me, and I felt as if I was in a fight for my life. Little did I know, I was. At one point, I stretched out on the bathroom floor and just laid there, thinking to myself. I'm in here dying and everybody else is sleeping. I managed to get back up and sat on the toilet with my head laying on the vanity, when I felt I was being watched. I raised my head and in the doorway stood this dark figure all in black and I knew it was the spirit of death. I could hardly raise my head I was so weak, so I said to the Lord in my Spirit - Lord, I know somewhere "You've got somebody praying for me." This was all inward for I was to weak to even open my mouth. The very next morning I got a phone call from a friend in Indiana saying, how the Lord had him up all night praying for me. When I couldn't fight God raised up someone to fight for me. He wanted me to know He heard the cry of my heart and He was with me through it all.

When my husband and the children got up the next morning they didn't even know I was in a fight for my life while they slept.

I went to my doctor who told me to go to the hospital immediately. I was pregnant and the baby was in my tube. My blood pressure was through the roof.

I came home told my husband what the doctor had said and that he had to get me to the hospital. Well, his response was he had to go to work and for me to get my girlfriend to take me. Well, I sort of lost it at that moment and yelled at him to say the least. To make a long story short, he took me to the hospital. The doctor came in to prepare me for surgery along with this nurse who was to give me this shot.

The shot she gave me I felt as if I had been kicked in the rear by a horse. Lying there, trying not to cry the Lord spoke and told me to apologize to my husband for the way I had yelled at him. I said, "Apologize to him", and of course, the answer was, "Yes!" I called him over to the bed and I told him how sorry I was for how I had yelled at him earlier. When I said those words it was as if a force hit him and knocked him back into his chair.

Suppose I had been stubborn or to proud to repent and say I was sorry, I could have died on that operating table.

Forgiveness is for you, not the other person. It is not an option; it is a command!

My husband never said, "Thank you or forgive me, I was wrong." Nothing, and it didn't even matter I did my part.

CHAPTER FOURTEEN
ANGELS UNAWARE

Revelation 12:11
And they overcame him by the blood of the lamb and by the world of their testimony and they loved not their lives to the death.

When my children were young, my oldest son was out playing one day when I heard that cry at the door that all mothers know that some thing is terribly wrong. I opened the door and there stood my son with his hand under his chin and blood was everywhere. While playing he had hit under his chin so hard, he bit his tongue and split his tongue at the tip in half. I remembered a testimony I had heard and I began go pray and command the bleeding to stop and that his tongue be healed in the Name of Jesus. Later that night, the children were all gathered around the TV and my husband was at work. All of a sudden, my son turned to me and asked if he could have an apple. Now remember, this is the same child who just a few hours ago, split his tongue. I looked up and said you want an apple? He said, "Yes!" I got up peeled him an apple cut it in slices and he ate the whole apple without flinching or even mentioning his tongue. God healed my son's tongue and wanted me to know it was done.

When my husband came in from work the children were all in bed and I couldn't wait to tell him what happened and how God healed our son's tongue. Well, he didn't see it that way and he had a fit. He said, "I should have called for the EMS," and I said, "Don't you get it?" God stopped the bleeding and healed him. He didn't want to hear that! So the next morning, we left taking him to Critteon Hospital for them to do nothing, but tell my son to stick out his tongue and tell us that the tongue was a different member and that when it completely healed, he would re-split it and they would put stitches in it. In my spirit, I said the devil is a liar, if he thinks he's going to re-split my son's tongue. As for my husband, when he saw that after every visit, it was costing him money, after 2 visits, he was finished with the doctor. The way the hospital was laid out, you went down a flight of narrow steps to the basement to see the doctor. The last time we left from seeing the doctor on the way going up the stairs from the basement was me first, my son, and my husband in a single file. Suddenly, the door opened and there stood this woman on her way down to the basement. She caught my attention, because when she saw me, her face lite up with the biggest smile and her eyes never left me. It was as if she knew me, which caused me to ask her, "Do I know you?" Still smiling she said, "No, but I know you and your husband, and we will meet again." She continued on down the stairs when it dawned on me that my son had left his hat and I went back down the stairs to get it. I looked for that lady everywhere and she was no where to be found. In my spirit, I felt I had an encounter with an angel. How did she know the man behind me was my husband? We were not together coming up the stairs. Remember, I went down behind her and the only way out was for her to come back up the stairs. It was as if, she vanished into thin air by the way, I just want you to know that God healed my son's tongue the day I prayed, and to proved it: when he asked for an apple. To this day he has not had a problem with his tongue and there has been no need for any type of surgery. Look at God!

Closing Thoughts:

In my obedience to put pen to paper I have gone through many changes and God has revealed himself to me in ways I can not even explain. I can tell you this - the Shirley that sat down to write this book is not the same, Shirley. Obedience is the key that will unlock the door into many of the secret things, the hidden things of God. I believe that many of the hidden things he shared with me, while writing this book I would not have known if I had not been obedient. The God we serve is not a complicated God, even though the enemy wants us to believe he is. In sharing parts of my journey, I pray you the readers have been stirred to stop putting off for tomorrow what God has told you to do today. Time is your enemy not your friend. You don't have the time you think you have, tomorrow just may be too late!

Hebrews 3:15
Today if you will hear his voice, do not harden your heart as in the rebellion.

WRITE THE BOOK!
BIRTH THE VISION!
PUSH!!!!!
EXCEPT THE CALL TO MINISTRY!
GET OUT OF THE BOAT!

You know He is talking to you, stop acting like **YOU DON'T HEAR!**

Coming to the end of this book this song came up into my spirit and I began to sing unto the Lord. "How can I say thanks for all the things you have done for me? Things so undeserved, yet you gave to prove your love for me. The voices of a million angels cannot express my gratitude. For all that I am or ever hoped to be, I owe it all to You!"

TO GOD BE THE GLORY!

ABOUT THE AUTHOR

Apostle Shirley Wharton is a mother of five, and grandmother of three. She is the Pastor and Apostle over God's Way Ministry. She is called to teach, train, and equip leadership for the work of the ministry. She is an intercessor and also called to teach others how to be led by the Holy Spirit. She received a Bachelor's degree from API and graduated in 2013. She can be seen every 2nd Sunday on Comcast channel 20 via Bell Global Network at 8am.

Contact Information:
shirleywarton@att.net
313-515-4877

www.ingramcontent.com/pod-product-compliance
Lightning Source LLC
Chambersburg PA
CBHW031637160426
43196CB00006B/456